Russian Poland

www.stickingplacebooks.com

© David Mamet 1993
© Sticking Place Books 2025

Cover design by Maria Wilk

ISBN 978-1-942782-99-5

Russian Poland

David Mamet

Sticking Place Books
New York

My grandmother, Clara, was from Hrubestow, a small city on the Bug River, the boundary, in the early 20th Century, between Poland and the Ukraine.

Hrubestow is 30 miles from the Polish city of Chelm, which, to the Polish Jews, was the locus of idiots. e.g. the Elders of Chelm petitioned God to correct his error, as He'd ordered the sun to shine by day, rather than by night, when it was needed.

Clara told me stories of the pogroms she'd survived in the Pale of Settlement — the area permitted to the Russian Jews. The Pale was geographically known as Volhynia, and known to her, and, then, to me, as Russian Poland.

The tales-within-the-tale, here, are fables of Isaac Luria, the Ari (lion) of Sfat, in the late 16th Century. Sfat, near the Galilee, was, in his lifetime, part of the Ottoman Syria, now part of the State of Israel.

I set his mystical tales in my grandmother's Volhynia, and framed them in another fable.

My friend Lou Lenart (1921–2015) was a Hungarian immigrant Jew. He enlisted in the Marine Corps in WWII and flew Corsairs in the Battle of Okinawa. After the war, he flew for the Sherut Avir, the precursor to the Israeli Air Force.

Lou was the commander of the four-plane Operation Pleshet (1948). The four planes were the totality of Israel's fighter capacity. They stopped the Egyptians outside Tel Aviv and saved the city.

Prior to the War of Independence, Lou flew interdicted aircraft and munitions from Europe to Israel; flights at the end of and beyond their range, landing on fumes.

The Fables of the Ari, here, are set in such a flight, as two pilots of Sherut Avir ferry the plane, arms, and a survivor of the Shoah to the new Jewish State, fighting for life.

David Mamet

Fade in.

Angle
EXT. Hillside.

Cliffs overlooking the sea. Day.

The Mediterranean below. A British Army jeep, with two men in uniform, pulls into the frame. Camera pans with them to reveal they are traveling along a line of high wire fence.

Angle
The jeep. Two young men in WWII-era RAF uniforms. A Sergeant driving, an Officer riding. They stop. The Sergeant nods and the Officer looks.

Angle
Their POV: a huge rent in the fence, in a small gully below.

Angle
The two men in the jeep. The Officer nods. The jeep pulls forward. Camera pans with the jeep as it moves slowly forward. Camera stops on a huge sign (in Italian and English) on the fence. The sign reads (first in Italian, then in English):

> YOU ARE WARNED. THIS IS AN INSTALLATION OF THE ROYAL AIR FORCE. KEEP OUT.

Angle
The jeep pulls over on the top of the gully and stops. The two men start down to the rent in the fence. As they come over the crest they see an Old Man, dressed in rags, looking out to sea. The two men change directions and come over to the Old Man. (The two men speak in clipped British accents. The Old Man speaks in a thick Eastern European accent).

> OFFICER
> What are you doing here? You speak English? What are you doing here?

The Old Man gestures out at the sea.

> OFFICER
> How long has that break in the fence been here?

The Old Man shrugs.

> OFFICER
> Have the patrols seen it? Have the patrols been by? You see the patrols from here?

> OLD MAN
> I see everything.

> OFFICER
> You do? You can see the patrols?

> OLD MAN
> I see them and I hear them.

> OFFICER
> What do they say?

> OLD MAN
> The password... (*he shrugs*)

> OFFICER
> Are they aware of the break in the fence? They say the *password*? In your hearing, you heard them?

The Officer exchanges a look with the Sergeant, who shakes his head, as if to say, "The old man's crazy."

> OFFICER
> What *is* the password, then?

                    OLD MAN
"Poppy."

                    OFFICER
"Poppy…"

He sighs.

                    OFFICER
What are you doing here?

The Old Man points over the sea.

                    OFFICER
There. Yes. What's over there.

                    OLD MAN
Palestine.

                    OFFICER
To "Palestine." And how're you going to get to Palestine?

                    OLD MAN
                    (gestures)
The planes.

                    OFFICER
The *planes*? There isn't a plane on the field with *near* that range.

The Old Man shrugs.

The Officer gestures to the Sergeant, who goes back to the jeep and takes it down the gully and, gingerly, through the rent in the fence. The Officer hangs back.

>   OFFICER
> And why'd you want to go there? Whose
> bloody country's going to war? The Arabs
> say they're going to drive you people into
> the sea. (*pause*) They're trying to kill you
> all. Don't you know that?

Pause.

The Old Man shrugs. The Officer looks at him for a moment. Sound of the Sergeant gunning the engine of the jeep. The Officer turns.

Angle
His POV: the Sergeant has maneuvered the jeep through the wire.

Angle
The Officer and the Old Man.

>   OFFICER
>   (*softly, to himself*)
>   They want to kill you all...

He turns away from the Old Man, who looks after him for a moment, then back at the sea. In the far B.G., on the hills by the cliffs, we see goats grazing.

Angle
At the jeep. The Officer climbing into the jeep. The rent in the fence behind him. The jeep starts to move.

Angle
Airfield. Day.
The jeep is on a runway. At the far end are hangars and maintenance sheds, and, in the far distance, a small control tower. The Officer looks at his watch, then at the Sergeant, who nods. The jeep leaves the frame.

Angle
Maintenance hangar. Day.
A man in coveralls holding a clipboard looks up at the sound of the approaching jeep. He moves toward the front of the hangar and we see the bomber he is working on. The coverall man goes out onto the tarmac as the jeep approaches.

>OFFICER
>Where's your commanding officer?

>MECHANIC
>I…

>OFFICER
>Who's in command here? Where's your security force?

The mechanic looks back. Out of a small office area, two soldiers with rifles double-time up to the group at the jeep.

>SOLDIER
>Password!

Angle
The two soldiers, standing near a large sign, white on black, which is in the process of being painted. The sign reads, in large block letters, "YOU ARE IN A RESTRICTED AR…" We see the last two letters, "EA" penciled in, and a bucket of white paint on a bench nearby, with a paintbrush sitting on it. The Officer steps into the shot.

>OFFICER
>*(to mechanic)*
>Where's your superior?

>SOLDIER
>Password!

OFFICER
The password's "Poppy," as it seems the
whole world knows. Stand down.

The Officer and the Sergeant, who has taken out a notepad, walk back into the hangar, where we see a small fighter-bomber. The mechanic follows them back into the hangar.

OFFICER
When was the last time you had a security
drill?

MECHANIC
Sir, I…

OFFICER
What shape is this aircraft in? Give me that…

He takes the clipboard and looks at it.

OFFICER
Isn't this…? Check me the tail number,
Sergeant. Is this aircraft listed as "combat
ready"?

MECHANIC
I…

OFFICER
Is it listed as "combat ready"?

MECHANIC
I… Sir, it just came off the flight line, there's
a small…

The Officer and the Sergeant start walking around the plane. The Officer looks out at the two soldiers on the tarmac over his shoulder.

                    OFFICER
      What are they gawking at? Put those men
      on report and have them report to base
      H.Q. Right now. Right now.

                    SERGEANT
      Sir!

He goes off with his notebook to talk to the guards. The
Officer continues walking around the plane.

                    OFFICER
      And what, have you told me, is the
      problem?

                    MECHANIC
      It's just a small…

He gestures, as if to say "If I might just have the clipboard
for a moment…" He takes the clipboard, and tries to call the
Officer's attention to it. The Officer pays him no attention.

In the B.G. we see the two soldiers, double-timing across the
field, away from the hangar. The Sergeant comes back inside.
The Officer shakes his head. He looks toward the control
tower.

Angle
His POV: the control tower. Several planes on the hardstand
near it. The sun is about to set.

Angle
The Sergeant and the Officer. The Officer sighs. Looks at his
watch. The Sergeant shrugs, as if to say "I don't understand
it either."

                    OFFICER
                  (to mechanic)
      You've signed off on this plane? Have
      you? Have you endorsed it? You tell me

> it's combat ready, and yet… What sort of a base do you *have* here? Do you know there's a *rent* in your fence, big enough to…

Sound of a huge explosion. All turn to look.

Angle
Beyond them, we see the control tower is on fire.

> MECHANIC
> *(under his breath)*
> *What* the hell?

Pause.

A siren goes off in the hangar.

> OFFICER
> *(under his breath)*
> Oh, Lord.

Angle
The Mechanic, holding the clipboard. He throws it into the plane.

> OFFICER
> Where's your fire station?

> MECHANIC
> *(points across the field)*
> It's back at the… I'm on the…

He nods at a bicycle against the wall of the hangar. The Officer nods "get going." The Mechanic bows a quick thanks to them, grabs a firehat off the wall, and starts pedaling away.

Angle
The control tower burning in the B.G. The Mechanic on the bike cycling away from the hangar. The Officer, the Sergeant and the plane in the foreground.

The Officer looks at his watch and wipes his forehead. The Sergeant shakes his head. The Officer climbs into the plane through a cargo door.

Angle
Inside the plane. A work-light hanging. The Officer steps on something.

Angle
INS. It is the clipboard the mechanic threw into the plane.

Angle
The Officer moving forward to the cockpit. He picks up the clipboard and flings it back into the cargo area. He moves forward.

Angle
C.U. He bumps his head on a lever, on which the work light is hanging. He takes down the work light, switches it off, and throws it back into the cargo area. Hold on the lever for a moment. A turncock, which reads: "MAIN TAKE ON, MAIN TAKE OFF."

Angle
Cockpit. The Officer sits in the right-hand seat. Takes off his hat and looks down at the controls.

Angle
His POV: the controls.

>   VOICE SHOUTING
>   *(in American English)*
>   Well, what about it?

Angle

The Officer, looking around. The shouter is the Sergeant, at the back of the hangar, unlocking the back hangar doors and rolling them open.

OFFICER
(now in American accent)
Yeah. I can fly it.

Beyond the now-open doors we see a high fence. A 1940s station wagon pulls up to it and beeps the horn. The Sergeant goes to the fence, taking wire cutters from the back of the jeep, and clips the lock. The station wagon drives through the fence and into the hangar, the Sergeant on the running board.

Angle

At the plane. The station wagon stops. Several men, dressed in 1940s work clothes, rough sport-coats and sweaters, get out and start hauling a large rubber tank toward the plane. One of them hands the Sergeant a Tommy gun. He stands by the door, looking out at the burning control tower across the field.

Angle

Cockpit. The Officer, trying various switches. He looks out at the burning tower and back into the cargo area as the sport-coated men carry the tank into the plane.

OFFICER
How is it out there?

MAN
(in Italian accent)
It'll burn for a while.

The Officer opens the window, levers himself up on the nose of the plane, and drops to the ground. He opens his tunic, showing American dog tags. Walks to the Sergeant, who is standing at the entrance to the hangar. The Sergeant looks at him.

                    OFFICER
                  (in response)
           It's a B-25. It's like a 25. It's a two-engine
           plane.

                    SERGEANT
           We gonna have the range?

                    OFFICER
           I figure if we get that tank full, we should
           have the range. Just.

                    SERGEANT
           Is the main tank full?

The Officer leans over and flicks a switch on the control panel.

Angle
INS. The fuel gauge. Reads "MAIN TANK FULL."

                   OFFICER (V.O.)
           The mechanic said he topped it off.

Angle
The two men in the cockpit.

                   OFFICER (V.O.)
           That, and the tank they're putting in.

The Sergeant reaches over and takes a pack of cigarettes from the T-shirt pocket of the officer.

                    OFFICER
           That's our last one. These boys're turning
           this plane into a gasoline bomb.

He gestures toward the men working in back.

Angle
The hangar. A large tank marked "PETROL/AVIATION." A man takes a hose and moves to the plane. Camera pans with him.

Angle
Two of the men are working on installing a huge rubber tank into the cargo hold. They look up. One motions "one second." The other man looks at his watch. Then the first man nods and the hose is passed up to him.

Angle
The gas tank.

> MAN IN PLANE
> *(calls, in Italian)*
> Okay. Turn it on.

The man at the tank throws a switch and we hear the hum of the pump.

Angle
The hangar. The Officer and the Sergeant look back at the plane. The Officer takes the cig from the Sergeant, takes a drag, and drops it on the tarmac.

Angle
His boot, rubbing the cig out. The two men walk away back into the hangar.

Angle
The hangar. The sport-coated men working at the tank.

> THE MAN INSIDE THE PLANE
> *(in Italian)*
> Okay. Shut it off. It's full.

The man outside calls the same message to the man at the pump. We hear the pump stop.

> MAN INSIDE
> I can't get out.

The Officer and the Sergeant walk back toward the plane. The man outside translates.

> MAN OUTSIDE
> (*in Italian-accented English*)
> He says he can't get out. He's trapped by the tank.

> OFFICER
> Tell 'em to come out by the nose.
> (*he gestures*)
> Out by the nose. Through the cockpit.
> (*he looks at his watch again*)
> (*to the Sergeant*)
> Let's get out of here.

The Officer passes to the wing. We see the cargo door being shut off and the man trapped inside, moving toward the nose. The Officer climbs up the wing, toward the cockpit.

Angle
The Sergeant, standing near the half-painted sign. He looks at it, takes the white paint and brush, and moves under the wing.

Angle
At the nose, the sport-coated man is helped out of the window by the officer. The Officer shakes hands and climbs into the right-hand seat.

Angle
Underneath the wing. The Sergeant painting.

Angle
INT. Cockpit.

The officer looks out. We see the Sergeant, with the paint bucket and brush, emerge from under the wing.

                    OFFICER
                 (*shouting down*)
        Chocks. And clear it, let's get out of here.

Angle
Inside the hangar. One man yelling in Italian and two other men pulling out the chocks. The Sergeant and one of the sport-coated man standing apart, talking. Another sport-coated man runs up and hands a large paper bag to the Sergeant.

Angle
Cockpit. The Officer yelling.

                    OFFICER
    Clear?

                    SERGEANT
                  (*looks around*)
    Clear.

                    OFFICER
    Let's go!

The sport-coated man hands the Sergeant back his Tommy gun. The number one engine is started. The sport-coated man converses with the Sergeant, pointing to the bag. The Sergeant nods. We do not hear their conversation over the sound of the engine.

The Sergeant flings away the bucket of paint and starts up the wing to the cockpit.

The Officer moves aside as the Sergeant comes in through the window.

Angle
The plane. The other engine is started, the plane starts to move out of the hangar. In the B.G. we see the sport-coated men rush back into the station wagon, which moves back through the fence.

Angle
Cockpit. The Sergeant strapping himself into his seat. He looks into the bag.

> SERGEANT
> Coffee. Lunch.

> OFFICER
> The maps?

The Sergeant extracts a road map. The Officer glances at it.

> OFFICER
> It's a *road map*.

> SERGEANT
> You got your radio, you got your compass, you fly eighty-five degrees, the Mediterranean, and that's…

He puts the map back in the paper bag.

> OFFICER
> Let's get outta here.

Angle
The plane taxiing in the sunset.

Angle
Longshot. The station wagon, moving quickly, on a dirt road, below it the airfield, the plane taxiing, the control tower, in the distance, burning.

Angle
Cockpit. The Sergeant takes out a handkerchief, wipes his hands.

                        OFFICER
                        (absently)
     What's that?

                        SERGEANT
     I got paint on my hands. You going to be
     able to lift this sucker off?

The Sergeant looks out of his window.

Angle
His POV: the control tower, the fire dying down.

Camera pans (as if the plane is moving), revealing the hillside and the Old Man sitting on it.

Angle
The plane.

The Officer circles it to start take-off procedures. He is now at the bottom of the runway. (NB: takeoff checklist to come.)

Halfway through the list, the officer looks out and sees the Old Man. The Sergeant glances back at the control tower.

Angle
His POV: trucks and a jeep coming back across the field.

                        SERGEANT
              We got about three minutes to…

He turns.

Angle
The Officer, looking out of the window.

Angle
His POV: the Old Man, looking back at him.

Angle
Switch. The control panel. The Officer's hand comes down and throws a switch.

Angle
The plane. The left engine dies and stops.

Angle
Cockpit. The Officer starts unbuckling his harness.

> SERGEANT
> We can't lift off as it is. We're overweight as it is.

> OFFICER
> *(climbing out of the nose of the plane)*
> Throw out the radio.

> SERGEANT
> Throw out the... How're we going to make landfall?

> OFFICER
> On the nose of the plane. Eight-five degrees... How can we miss?

Angle
The Officer running toward the break in the fence.

Angle
Cockpit. The Sergeant, using a small bicycle wrench, ripping out the large radio.

Angle
The Old Man. The Officer talking to him. The Old Man rises. The sea beyond. The Old Man looks toward the plane.

Angle
His POV: the plane.

Angle
Cockpit. The Sergeant tearing out the radio. He wrenches it out of the control panel. He looks down.

Angle
His POV: the Old Man, being helped to the plane by the Officer. The Old Man starts to open the cargo door. The Officer helps him onto the wing.

Angle
At the top of the wing. The Sergeant, coming out of the small window. He hauls the radio up after him and sets it on the wing. He reaches his hand down for the Old Man and helps him into the window.

SERGEANT
In the back. Let's go.

Angle
C.U. The Old Man, looking around, wonderingly, gets into the plane. The Sergeant heaves the radio down onto the tarmac.

Angle
INS. The radio hitting the tarmac. Above is the Sergeant, getting into the plane. The Officer following him.

Angle
Cockpit. The Officer and the Sergeant, and the Old Man, behind them, moving back into the plane. The Old Man brushes his head on the fuel cock.

SERGEANT
Sit down and hold on.

The Old Man nods and sits in the cramped space. The Officer moves forward a throttle.

Angle
EXT. The plane.

The left engine starts up.

> OFFICER
> Well, this is going to be interesting.

> SERGEANT
> Can you lift it off?

> OFFICER
> Anything you can think to throw it, do it now.

Angle
The Officer's hands on the control yoke, moving the throttles forward.

Angle
The Sergeant looks around, throws out two parachutes, throws out the paper sack with lunch. He hesitates, then throws out the Tommy gun.

Angle
C.U. The Old Man, in the back, looking on.

Angle
The Officer and the Sergeant.

> OFFICER
> Here we go.

The Sergeant thinks a moment, then takes the small bicycle wrench out of his shirt pocket and throws it away. The Officer moves the throttles forward.

Angle
The wheels of the plane begin to roll.

                    SERGEANT
          Happens if we abort?

                    OFFICER
          We don't abort. This plane's a flying fuel
          tank. We're gonna fly or we're gonna burn.
          Call it out...

                    SERGEANT
          Forty-forty-five...

Angle
INS. The airspeed indicator. The Officer's hands, moving the throttles forward.

Angle
The Officer and the Sergeant.

                    SERGEANT
          What speed do we rotate at?

                    OFFICER
          It's like the B-25. We fly at 110, but with
          this load... Call it out...

                    SERGEANT
          Sixty-sixty-five.

Angle
A stretch of runway. The plane's undercarriage comes into it, then leaves the shot, leaving the dying flames of the control tower beyond.

Angle
INT. The plane.

C.U. The Officer.

> SERGEANT (VO)
> Eighty-eighty-five… (*pause*) Eighty…

The Officer looks ahead.

Angle
His POV: the end of the runway, cliffs and the sea beyond, the plane gaining on them.

Angle
INT. The cockpit.

The Officer glances quickly down at the airspeed.

Angle
INS. The airspeed indicator hovers just above eighty.

Angle
The Officer and the Sergeant. The Sergeant looking down.

> SERGEANT
> Eighty-eighty off…

He looks up.

Angle
His POV: the end of the runway coming closer.

Angle
From the front. The two men, with the Old Man in the back. The plane comes toward camera and departs.

Angle
INT. The cockpit.

> SERGEANT
> (*looking down*)
> Eighty-five… She ain't going to fly.

> OFFICER:
> I'm gonna put her over the cliff... Hang on...

Angle
The plane, speeding down the runway.

Angle
The verge of the runway, the tarmac meets the grass. The plane leaves the tarmac and starts onto the grass.

Angle
INT. Cockpit.

The three men. The plane bumping over the grass.

Angle
The edge of the cliff, seen from below. The plane looms up into the shot as the camera rises, to show the runway, the fire far in the B.G. The plane falls out of the shot.

Angle
INT. The plane.

Angle
C.U. The Old Man, looking forward.

Angle
His POV: the backs of the two men, the sea coming up beyond them.

> SERGEANT
> Ninety-ninety-five...

Angle
The face of the cliff. The wing of the plane falling through the shot.

Angle
The Officer. He flicks a glance at the airspeed indicator.

Angle
His POV: it hovers just at 110.

Angle
INS. The Officer's hands on the wheel. He pulls it back toward him.

Angle
The surface of the sea, waves lapping. The underbelly of the plane as it skims the waves.

Angle
INT. The plane.

The Officer pulling back on the wheel.

Angle
The sky. The plane rises through the shot. Leaves the shot and we tilt down to see the airfield, growing small, in the B.G.

Angle
To clifftop. A goat grazing looks up.

Angle
INT. The plane.

Three men. The Officer flicking switches on the control panel.

>   OFFICER
>   *(to Sergeant)*
>   You keep a close eye on that auxiliary tank.
>   When it goes, we switch over to the main
>   fuel.

The Sergeant nods. Turns around, glances back at the tank.

Camera pans with him. We see the small fuel gauge on the rubber tank and the Old Man.

OLD MAN
Where are we going?

Angle
EXT. The plane.

As it starts to bank, revealed is the underside of one wing, on which is crudely painted, in white paint, a Star of David.

Dissolve.

Angle
EXT. The plane.

Pan off of clouds in the sky, a shadow of the plane, then onto the plane.

Angle
INT. The plane.

The officer checking the control panel.

SERGEANT
You got it in trim?

OFFICER
I think so.

SERGEANT
Keep it lean.

OFFICER
Lean as a bean. Gimme the maps. You take it.

He relinquishes the wheel.

                    SERGEANT
    Heading?

                    OFFICER
    Eight-five degrees.

The Officer starts looking around. He turns back to the Old Man.

                    OFFICER
    How you doing?

The Old Man smiles. The Officer smiles back.

                    OLD MAN
    We're going to Palestine.

                    OFFICER
    God willing and weather permitting…
            (to Sergeant)
    That's where we're going… Where are the maps?

The Sergeant looks around.

Beat.

                    SERGEANT
    I tossed 'em.

Beat.

Hold on the two men. The Officer nods. Takes out a pencil and starts figuring on a notebook he takes from the Sergeant's tunic.

                    OFFICER
    We fly eight-five degrees, eleven.

> SERGEANT
> That going to take us there?

> OFFICER
> It's going to take us somewhere…

> SERGEANT
> Well, look, look, we make land, we radio…

He looks down.

Angle
His POV: the empty space where the radio was, wires protruding.

Angle
The Officer and the Sergeant. Pause. The Officer shrugs. He opens his tunic and takes out a crumpled Air Force "FIFTY MISSIONS" hat and puts it on.

> SERGEANT
> A little bit of sentiment, eh?

The Sergeant takes out the pack of cigarettes from his shirt and starts to light up.

> OFFICER
> Can't smoke it.

The Sergeant puts the pack away.

> SERGEANT
> Can't smoke, and I'm afraid I chucked our
> coffee. Going to be a long flight.

The Officer turns back to the Old Man.

> OFFICER
> It's going to be a while. You want to get
> some sleep?

> OLD MAN
> I don't think so, no thank you.

> OFFICER
> *(pause)*
> You ever flown before?

> OLD MAN
> In my dreams.

The Officer nods.

Pause.

> OLD MAN
> I *flew*… I saw things… In my village…

The Officer smiles. The Old Man fidgets.

> OFFICER
> You uncomfortable?

> OLD MAN
> No. It's nothing.

Pause.

> OFFICER
> You sure?

> OLD MAN
> It's nothing.

The Old Man's look drifts away. The Officer turns back to the controls, checks them. Turns back to the Old Man.

> OFFICER
> You were saying… In your village…?

The Old Man turns back to him.

> OLD MAN
> In my village… (*pause*) Long ago… (*pause*)
> Many things… (*pause*) There was a man…
> There was a man… (*pause*) There was a
> poor beggar…

Angle
C.U. The Officer, turned around, listening,

> OLD MAN
> And he would beg at the shul…

Dissolve.

Angle
EXT. Eastern village.

A longshot. A road on a hill. A Beggar comes into the shot, moving across the frame left to right. A mullioned window bangs into the shot. Camera pulls back slightly to reveal we have been looking at the scene through a window. The window frame bangs in the wind.

Angle
EXT. Shul. Day.

The Rabbi, in a shtetl costume of the 1890s, talking to several people coming to shul.

> RABBI
> (*to the group*)
> Money and labor to keep the shul in *repair*,
> then it falls into *disrepair*. It's a foreseeable
> process.

He pries a piece of rotting clapboard from the wall and lifts it to show it to the assembled people. Sound of the window flapping. Rabbi turns to look and gestures at the window, as an example of what he has been discussing.

Angle
His POV: the hill. The window flapping beyond it. The Beggar we saw previously on the hill.

Angle
On the hill, the Beggar passes a young woman, who is sitting on a rock, looking at him. She nods, he nods, he continues walking. Below him, down the hill, we see the shtetl. Several low wooden buildings, the shul, with the Rabbi and several Congregants outside it. The Beggar sighs and starts down the hill.

Angle
Down the hill. Two Housewives, walking with their families, toward the shul, the Beggar in the B.G.

> HOUSEWIFE ONE
> …which I stitched with the same thread that I did the smocking with.

> HOUSEWIFE TWO
> I want to see it.

> HOUSEWIFE ONE
> Of course you want to see it, that's why I brought it with me. (*she gestures to a small package which she holds under her arm*) And who is going to be the loveliest bride within the memory of living man?

The Housewife gestures behind her, to a young woman. The Beggar comes into the frame.

> BEGGAR
> Balabusteh… Can you help me? Can you help a poor man? In honor of your

daughter and the upcoming event? Such a
lovely girl... in honor of your daughter.

The Housewife reaches into her purse, scrounges through it, and passes the Beggar a coin.

> BEGGAR
> May you live a hundred and twenty years,
> and may every day of every one of those
> years...

Angle
The Beggar and the women in the B.G. The Rabbi and the Congregants in the foreground. In the B.G. we see the Beggar, bowing, start to leave the group and move toward the Rabbi. One of the Housewives starts to unwrap her package and display a piece of goods.

> RABBI
> ...where it is written, you see, that,
> doubting the *authority*, doubting the
> *authority* of Moses, which is why she
> turned leprous in the first place.

The Beggar comes up to the Rabbi.

> BEGGAR
> Rabbi...

> RABBI
> A pleasure to see you in the vicinity.

> BEGGAR
> Rabbi, my wife and family have no bread.

> RABBI
> What did I just see you put in your pocket?
> It looked like a coin.

                    BEGGAR
Indeed. It was a coin, and just sufficient for
tonight. And, as head of the house, I look
toward *tomorrow*, and those under my
care, and I think…

                    RABBI
And while you think I will remind you of
the Manna in the desert, where the holy
one, blessed be his name, caused it to fall
and *admonished* us not to collect more than
one day's needs, and to trust in him…

                    BEGGAR
Blessed be his name.

                    RABBI
Amen, that more would fall *tomorrow*.

As the Rabbi speaks, the Beggar turns his head to look at something.

Angle
His POV: on the far side of the shul, a Rich Man in a fur coat, mounted on a fine horse, rides, in a stately fashion, up to the shul.

                    RABBI (V.O.)
And you may recall that there were those,
not *trusting* in the divine words, who
sought to supply themselves with a *greater*
portion than…

Angle
The far side of the shul. The Rich Man, descending from his horse. Several of the members of the congregation reach out to help him. They bow to him. He reaches up to his saddlebags.

Angle
INS. The saddlebags, out of which comes a pillow.

Angle
The Rich Man, nodding to those around him, starts toward the shul.

Angle
Two Housewives, one showing the piece of fabric to the other.

> HOUSEWIFE ONE
> Spun with my very own hands.

> HOUSEWIFE TWO
> *(feeling the fabric)*
> And how do you get it so soft?

Camera pans off the Housewives onto the Beggar and Rabbi.

> RABBI
> …which is why we are told that the Manna began to stink in the nostrils, and, beyond being unfit to *eat*, would cause, in those who strove to partake of it…

> BEGGAR
> Thank you, Rabbi, would you excuse me?

Angle
The Beggar runs toward the shul.

Angle
The Rabbi calling after him.

> RABBI
> Where are you running?

                    BEGGAR
    …I…

                    RABBI
    Don't you use the shul for a shortcut. What
    is it? A *field*? And is it not written in *The
    Talmud*? If you walk through the house of
    prayer, *say* a prayer.

Angle
INT. Shul.

The Beggar, hurrying into the shul from outside. Stops in front of the ark.

                    BEGGAR
    Blessed are you Lord our God, king of the
    universe…

He hurries to the other side of the shul, where the Rich Man is just coming in.

                    BEGGAR
    Reb Siegel… Reb Siegel… What am I
    called? Tsedaka and Rachmones. Have pity
    on me… if you would, a poor man…

            REB SIEGEL (THE RICH MAN)
                (*gesturing, as if to say,
                "Don't embarrass yourself…"*)
    Not in the shul…

Reb Siegel walks into the shul with his pillow.

Angle
INT. Shul.

The Congregants entering the shul, the women going upstairs. Various Congregants make way for Reb Siegel, who goes to his seat by the wall and settles himself down with his pillow. The Rabbi goes to the front of the congregation and begins to put on his prayer shawl.

Angle
Two Old Men, at the back of the room, praying as they put on their prayer shawls. As they continue their prayers they turn, in a practiced motion, to look behind them, where we see Reb Siegel, who has fallen asleep. The two Old Men nod to each other, as if to say, "Right on time, everything is right with the world."

Behind the head of the sleeping Reb Siegel, the broken window is swinging in the wind. Beyond that, outside, the Two Housewives are gossiping.

Angle
EXT. Shul.

The Beggar is walking, dejectedly, around the shul. Camera tracks with him. He sits, with a sigh, on a rock. Wind is blowing the tree behind him. He gets a speck in his eye and extracts it.

Angle
The Two Housewives gossiping, the Beggar in the background.

Angle
INT. Shul.

The Torah is placed on a table and unrolled. The Rabbi calls someone up to read from the Torah.

Angle
The pointer on the Torah parchment.

Angle
Reb Siegel, sleeping soundly.

Angle
The reader:

> **READER**
> And the lord spoke to Moses saying, You must command the Children of Israel, and tell them that they bring to thee pure olive oil for the lamp, to cause a lamp to burn continually…

Angle
The two Old Men. Reb Siegel sleeping behind them.

> **READER (V.O.)**
> …And that the lamp shall burn continually outside the Tabernacle. And Aaron shall order it from evening to morning…

Angle
EXT. Shul.

The two gossiping Housewives. One has taken the white dress completely out of the wrapping and is holding it up to be admired. The broken window is flapping just beyond them. We hear the reader continuing.

> **READER (V.O.)**
> …And shall stand as a commandment forever…

Angle
INT. Shul.

Reb Siegel sleeping. The window is blowing in the breeze.

> **READER (V.O.)**
> …throughout all generations.

The window bangs behind Reb Siegel. He snuggles further down into a comfortable position. The prayer shawl works its way up over his head and down over his eyes.

Angle
Beyond him. The Housewives, holding up the white dress. The window is blown shut with a very loud bang.

Angle
The Two Old Men half turn at the sound.

Angle
Reb Siegel, under his prayer shawl, coming awake, trying to orient himself. He looks around.

Angle
His POV: through the screen of the prayer shawl, beyond the window, the disembodied form of the white dress being held in the air, and backlit, glowing.

> READER (V.O.)
> ...And you shall take fine flour, and bake twelve cakes with it...

Angle
X.C.U. Reb Seigel. He is confused and blinks his eyes. He looks again out of the window.

Angle
His POV: out the window. The dress, which now appears to be pointing at him.

> READER (V.O.)
> ...and two parts of an ephah shall be in each cake. And you shall set them in two rows, six in a row, upon the table before the Lord...

Angle
X.C.U. Reb Siegel.

> READER (V.O.)
> ...and every Sabbath day shall you do so,
> continually...

Angle
POV: the dress. Pointing at him. The dress is lowered from the window and replaced with a large expanse of light.

Angle
Reb Siegel, as the reader goes on.

> READER (V.O.)
> ...And it shall be an everlasting covenant...

The voice grows dimmer as Reb Siegel rubs his eyes and resubsides into sleep.

> READER (V.O.)
> ...And it shall be for Aaron and the sons of
> Aaron, and they shall partake of it in a holy
> place...

Reb Siegel yawns and falls back asleep.

Fade out.

Fade in.

Angle
EXT. Shul. Day.

Congregants issuing forth, chatting with the Rabbi, who glances inside.

Angle
POV: the last few people issuing from the shul, Reb Siegel asleep at the back.

Fade out.

Fade in.

Angle
INT. Reb Siegel's home.

A well-appointed home. A maid takes Reb Siegel's coat and hat. Bows as he comes into the front hall. He walks distractedly past her.

Angle
INT. Kitchen. Day.

Reb Siegel's wife with a Cook and a Maid.

> MRS. SIEGEL
> When you bake the bread. It is important, yes, that it is *bread*, and it, frankly, is as important that it is *good* bread…

Mrs. Siegel turns as Reb Siegel comes into the kitchen.

> MRS. SIEGEL
> Gut Shabbes… (*to maid*) See does the man want a glass of tea.

Angle
C.U. Reb Siegel, sitting down.

> MAID (V.O.)
> Would you like a glass of tea, sir?

Reb Siegel turns to look at her, looks away.

> MRS. SIEGEL (V.O.)
> Because, frankly, if I want it to taste like *clay*, and some mixture of clay and *wood*, I can bake it myself.

MAID (V.O.)
Sir, do you want a glass of tea…?

Reb Siegel turns to look at her.

Angle
His POV: her shape, in a white dress, backlit and outlined by the light from the window beyond her.

MRS. SIEGEL (V.O.)
If you bake. Ten or twelve loaves, during the week. That is your chance, do you see? To *excel.* We require twelve loaves of *good* bread…

Angle
Reb Siegel, as he stands.

MRS. SIEGEL (V.O.)
The purpose of such bread, to *sustain* us… to…

REB SIEGEL
I saw God. (*pause*) God spoke to me.

Pause.

He starts to exit, hurriedly.

Angle
EXT. Bakery. Shtetl street. Day.

Reb Siegel, leaving the bakery with twelve loaves of bread in his arms.

Angle
INT. Shul. Day.

The shul is empty. Camera tracks to the window, through which we see the Beggar, asleep, seated against a tree.

Reb Siegel hurrying into the shul.

Angle
Reb Siegel coming into the shul. He looks around. Proceeds up to the ark.

Beat.

REB SIEGEL
I am a bad man.

Beat.

> I know that it is said that poverty becomes a Jew, as a red bridle becomes a white horse. I am not poor. I am not learned. I come to the shul and sleep. I cannot read one word of Torah. (*pause*) I am a businessman. But, God. One thing that I know. One thing I know. And I have made my fortune from it. I know how to command. I know the sound of a command. And I have been commanded, and I do obey. *Take* my poor offering. *Take* this bread. God. *Take* it. Thank you. *Thank* you. For speaking to me.

He opens the ark.

Angle.
The ark. The Torah inside it.

REB SIEGEL
> I, who am nothing. I who am less than nothing…

Angle
The inside of the ark. The Torah. Reb Siegel's hands.

Arranging the bread in two rows of six loaves each. The bread is still hot and steaming.

> REB SIEGEL
> How great is your goodness. Who would speak to me.

Angle
Reb Siegel at the ark.

> REB SIEGEL
> Who would notice me. Thank you. *Thank* you. Here is your bread. Fresh. Hot from the oven, Lord. Thank you.

Reb Siegel closes the door of the ark and steps back.

Beat.

Angle
EXT. Shul. Day

Reb Siegel walking away from the shul.

Angle
The Beggar asleep against the tree. A fly buzzes at his face. He swipes at it and wakes up.

Angle
His POV: Reb Siegel, walking away from the shul.

Angle
The Beggar hurrying toward Reb Siegel. He comes to the corner of the shul and starts into the shul, as a shortcut. The Rabbi, who is talking with several parishioners, shouts after him.

> RABBI
> What are you doing…?

The Beggar gestures that he is cutting through the shul.

> RABBI
> No. You want to use the shul as a cross-roads? If you go into the shul, you pray…

Angle
INT. Shul.

The Beggar, hurrying inside, muttering to himself.

> BEGGAR
> I have to pray. Thank you for the regulation. Thank you for such drastic care of my life.

He stops in front of the ark to pray.

> BEGGAR
> Thank you for my life as a beggar, but I'm rather busy now, as somebody has to put food on my table, or the little ones starve, you see they have no bread…

He starts to hurry away from the ark and stops for a moment.

Angle
His POV: the ark. Steam from the bread is issuing from it.

Angle
The Beggar and the ark. He goes to the ark. Opens it.

Angle
C.U. The Beggar, looking down at the bread.

Beat.

A tear forms in his eye.

Angle
EXT. Shul.

Reb Siegel, at his horse, putting his pillow into the saddlebags. As he puts in the empty bread bag, the Rabbi accosts him.

> RABBI
> We have to make *sacrifices*, and, whom do we turn to, if not to you? The *building* is in disrepair.

Reb Siegel reaches in his pocket and hands bills to the Rabbi.

> REB SIEGEL
> I understand about sacrifices, Rabbi. I may not be *learned*…

> RABBI
> They are honored who study the Torah, and they are honored who *allow* them to st…

> REB SIEGEL
> I may not be learned, but I know what God calls on us to sacrifice, to offer up.

> RABBI
> Not to offer up, not to offer *up*, to offer to those *around* us. In the old days, *yes*. The sacrifice was meal, or flesh, upon the altar, but today…

> REB SIEGEL
> But we can sacrifice upon an altar *today*…

> RABBI
> Certainly not…

                   REB SIEGEL
        But if we have been *commanded* to..?

                     RABBI
        Certainly not. By whom?

Reb Siegel starts back to the shul.

                     RABBI
        But the *true* sacrifice. The true sacrifice…
               (he gestures to money)
        …is your support of the… Where are you
        going…?

Reb Siegel takes the bread bag out of his saddlebags.

                   REB SIEGEL
        I'm correcting a mistake.

Angle
INT. Shul.

Reb Siegel is entering the shul. He goes up to the altar and opens it. He opens his bread bag and looks toward the altar.

Angle
POV: the ark. Several Torahs but no bread.

Angle
Reb Siegel.

                   REB SIEGEL
                     (pause)
        You do exist. You exist and I doubted you.

He steps back. Through the window we see the Beggar in the B.G., distributing the bread to his family.

> REB SIEGEL
> You exist... Of *course* you exist. Who else but you made the world. You like that bread? You think *that's* challah? Wait till *next* week, and see what you get. You like raisins?

He closes the doors of the ark and backs away from it.

Angle
EXT. Shul.

Reb Siegel, coming out of the shul, the Beggar and his family in the B.G., walking away with the bread.

Fade out.

Fade in.

Angle
INT. Shul. Night.

The Bride, wearing the wedding dress we saw previously. Standing next to her the Groom. The Rabbi blessing them.

> RABBI
> The Lord bless you and keep you, and grant you peace.

Angle
Members of the congregation throwing candy at the Bride and Groom, and shouting "mazeltov" as they step down from the platform.

Angle
EXT. Shul.

The Bride and Groom, the Rabbi, and the rest of the Congregation coming out of the shul in the B.G.

Angle
Reb Siegel, with his bag of bread, looking on and smiling.

Angle
INT. Shul

The Shammes, extinguishing the lights and sweeping up the candy.

Angle
Reb Siegel, hurrying toward the shul with his bag of bread, the shul in the foreground, as the Shammes, extinguishing the final light, exits the shul.

Angle
INT. The deserted shul.

Reb Siegel entering with the bread bag, puts it down, takes a prayerbook from his pocket, and reads with difficulty.

> REB SIEGEL
> Praised be you, Lord our God, King of the universe, who brings forth bread from the Earth.

He gestures toward his bread, and starts toward the altar.

Beat.

> REB SIEGEL
> Each of us must serve as commanded.
> (*beat*) You're right.

Angle
EXT. Shul. Night.

The Beggar and his family. They are exhorting him to do something. He nods "Alright" and turns toward the camera.

Angle
EXT. Shul.

The empty bread bag swinging. The camera tracks it to Reb Siegel's horse. He mounts his horse. In the B.G. we see the Beggar entering the shul, tentatively.

Angle
INT. Shul. Night.

BEGGAR
Lord. Lord, once again, you find me here.
I have nothing to offer, and I have no merit.
But once again, my *family*…

Angle
EXT. Shul. Night.

The Beggar's family, waiting, their faces light up.

Angle
Their POV: the Beggar, hurrying toward them, away from the shul, his arms full of bread.

Fade out.

Fade in.

The broken window, almost off its hinges, swinging in the wind. It falls off the hinges.

Angle
INT. Shul.

The Rabbi looks up at the sound.

Angle
The wedding dress. Pullback to show the woman in the wedding dress, now thirteen years older, and pregnant, and

her husband next to her and a young boy standing in front of them, whom the Rabbi is blessing.

Angle
Reb Siegel, thirteen years older than when last we saw him, asleep. Two Old Men in front of him.

> RABBI (V.O.)
> Lift up his countenance to shine upon you, and grant you *peace*...

On the word "peace" the two Old Men look around to see Reb Siegel, who wakes up on the word "peace." The two Old Men nod to each other.

Angle
INT. Beggar's hut.

The Beggar leaving his hut. His wife calls after him. He turns back. She hands him a bag for the bread. He takes it and starts away from her.

Angle
EXT. Shul. Night.

The wedding dress woman, her husband, and several children, walking away from the shul, talking.

Angle
The now tattered bread bag, on Reb Siegel's horse. Reb Siegel and the Rabbi come up to it. We see the wedding dress woman in the B.G., walking home with her family. The Rabbi holds the window frame with the dangling hinges.

> RABBI
> *(to Reb Siegel)*
> Why your assistance is so *especially* needed at this time.

Reb Siegel goes in his pocket and hands some coins to the Rabbi.

> RABBI
> Good, excellent.

> REB SIEGEL
> *(philosophically)*
> A building decays.

> RABBI
> Does it not… You're going home, you're late. Gut Shabbes.

> REB SIEGEL
> Rabbi, gut Shabbes.

The Rabbi starts away, holding the window frame.

Angle
INT. Shul.

> BEGGAR
> What have I done? What is it I have done? Command me, and I shall be led…

Angle
POV: the empty ark. Only the Torahs, no bread. The Beggar standing in front of it.

> BEGGAR
> What have I done to offend you, my God? That you now deprive my children of bread?

Angle
The door to the shul opens. Reb Siegel standing there with the bread bag.

BEGGAR (V.O.)
Turn me from my wicked ways, turn me,
but do not *desert* me.

Reb Siegel starts toward the ark.

Camera pans with him.

Reb Siegel stands by the ark, checks his watch, shrugs, as the Beggar laments.

Beat.

Reb Siegel starts placing the loaves in the ark.

Beat.

The Beggar looks at him.

Angle
EXT. Shul, seen through the now paneless window.

The Rabbi, hurrying with the pane of glass. Camera pans with him to the shul and starts toward the frame, to place the window in it. He turns at the sound of the two men talking.

Angle
At the front of the shul, the two men, the bread between them in a sack. The Rabbi walks toward the front of the shul. The two men start explaining their dilemma to him. Reb Siegel takes a loaf out of the sack and gestures with it. The Rabbi still holds the window frame. Reb Siegel takes the twelve loaves and places them, in demonstration, inside the ark.

Angle
The Rabbi.

RABBI
A case of a *misunderstanding*. It's founded
on a *coincidence*, and a mishearing of the

text. But God... *God*, yes, he demands *sacrifice*, but not of this sort. This is *superstition*. It's a kind of...

Angle
INT. The Beggar's hut.

His wife and children looking expectantly at the door.

Angle
The bread bag, full, being carried along. It is hoisted up onto the horse. Reb Siegel mounts.

Angle
EXT. The Beggar's hut. Night.

The Beggar, empty handed, walking home.

Angle
The Rabbi, walking home, holding the windowpane, the shul in the B.G. He glances at the pane. Turns, sighs, and walks back toward the shul. In the B.G. we see Reb Siegel riding home. The Rabbi turns back toward the shul. Camera tracks back before him. His eyes widen. He sees something.

Angle
His POV: the Young Girl we saw on the wagon at the beginning of the story, standing between him and the shul.

Camera moves in to her. The Rabbi moves into the shot.

Beat.

YOUNG GIRL
There is someone who needs to see you.

Beat.

She gestures. The Rabbi moves off with her.

Angle
EXT. Forest. Night.

The pane of glass, moving through the woods, large in the frame, moonlight glancing off of it.

Angle
C.U. Rabbi.

He looks up.

Angle
His POV: before him, the Young Girl, moving through the woods, looks back at him.

Angle
From a high angle, a clearing. The Young Girl, then the Rabbi, move out into the moonlit.

Angle
The two, moving toward the camera. The Young Girl stops, motions the Rabbi that he must continue by himself. He turns.

Angle
POV: a cave, firelight within.

Angle
INS. The Rabbi puts down the pane of glass on a rock. The Young Girl is in the B.G.

The Rabbi starts forward.

Angle
EXT. The cave.

The Rabbi walks up to the mouth of the cave. Looks within. He moves forward.

Angle
X.C.U. The Young Girl looking on.

Angle
INT. The cave. Night.

A Hebrew manuscript open on a round wooden table. A man's hand marks his place and closes the manuscript.

Angle
C.U. The man, an Old Man with a rough beard, covered in a blanket.

Beat.

> OLD MAN
> I had a vision. In which I saw you.
> *(beat)* And, in the vision, I saw that you
> explained…What could not be explained.
> And, because you did so, you stopped
> *(beat)* a game. *(beat)* You stopped God's
> game, if you will. *(beat)* And, in my dream,
> I saw that, as you stopped God's game, that
> now you'd have to die.

Beat.

Angle
The Rabbi, and the Old Man beyond him, in the firelight.

Angle
C.U. The Rabbi.

Angle
C.U. The Young Girl, in the forest, looking on.

Angle
Her POV: the mouth of the cave. The Rabbi, exiting the cave, walks into the clearing.

Angle
INS. The rock, with the broken window on top of it. The Rabbi walks toward it, to pick it up.

Angle
The clearing. The Rabbi picking up the window frame. A flash of white light.

Angle
The Rabbi's hand, dropping the frame of glass onto the rock, where the remaining glass shatters.

Angle
The empty clearing.

We hear the sound of wind rustling leaves. A branch is whipped into the frame in the foreground. The clearing in the B.G. The sound of leaves in the wind mixes with the engine of the plane.

Angle
INT. The plane.

The Officer. Camera pans to take in the Sergeant, who is now flying the plane as the Sergeant moves the throttles.

> SERGEANT
> I'm on top of it.

Angle
INS. The Sergeant's hands on the throttles. The sound of the engines evens out.

Angle
The Officer, turning back into his chair.

> OFFICER
> How are we?

> SERGEANT
> Still on our auxiliary tank. Haven't switched onto the plane's regular tank yet. You want 'er?

OFFICER
In a minute…

He rubs his eyes.

SERGEANT
Why'nt you take a nap? Get some sleep. I'll call you in (*he glances at his watch*) two hours.

Pause.

The Officer settles down into his chair. Tilts his head over his eyes.

Pause

Angle
The Old Man, in the cramped space. He is fidgeting.

Pause.

OLD MAN
Where are you from?

SERGEANT
Where are we from? (*he looks at the recumbent Officer, who smiles*) Well, we're from "over there."

OLD MAN
And why are you going to Palestine?

Pause.

SERGEANT
Why are we going to Palestine? We're going to Palestine to fight. (*pause*) To fight in the war.

OLD MAN
And you've fought before.

Pause

SERGEANT
Hmm?

OLD MAN
You've fought before.

Pause.

The Sergeant, somber, looks over at the Officer, who is now asleep. He looks back.

Angle
The Sergeant, flying the plane. The Old Man behind him.

SERGEANT
Tell me about your village.

OLD MAN
What?

SERGEANT
About your village.

OLD MAN
Yes. It's gone. (*pause*)

SERGEANT
I know.

Pause.

OLD MAN
In the old days, though… In the old days…

The Old Man turns away, putting his face near the window, and speaks softly, as if to himself.

> OLD MAN
> In the old days… We had people there. Some of whom were renowned. For goodness. For wisdom. (*pause*) For learning. And one man, Rebbe… The "Old Rebbe," in particular…

Angle
EXT. Small wooden house. Night. Everything covered in snow.

A young Boy leading a goat past the house in the small shtetl. He turns to look in the window, where we see a glow.

Angle
His POV: in the small house, an old, gnarled Rebbe, bent over a text, reading by candlelight.

> OLD MAN (V.O.)
> …had the power. To reduce most things. To make them *plain*.

Angle
INT. The house.

A page of Talmud. The Rebbe's hand comes through the frame and we travel with it to a glass of tea and beyond that. A small pot of jam. The Rebbe's hand takes a spoon out of the jampot and puts the spoonful of jam into the tea.

Angle
The Rebbe, drinking the tea. Beyond him, in the fireplace, a dying fire. He looks down at the text and gestures to it, as if in conversation with it. Then he opens another text and looks for the correct page, and gestures, as if to call the attention of the first text to the existence of the second. He sighs and

takes a sip of tea. He closes first one text and then the other, and moves them aside. He takes down a box from a bookshelf and removes tefillin, then says the prayers, as he starts to wrap himself in them.

There is a banging on the door. The Rebbe continues to pray. The banging intensifies.

Pause.

The Rebbe starts taking off his tefillin. He moves to the window and looks out.

Angle
His POV: outside is a richly appointed sleigh, draped in furs. Harness and bells gleaming. A fur-hatted Coachman sitting up front. The banging intensifies.

Angle
The crooked door. The Rebbe comes into the frame. He opens the door. In the door stands a large, distraught man, covered in furs.

Angle
The Rebbe, looking on, wonderingly. The man comes into the shot and they both stand in the open doorway.

> RICH MAN
> I want to repent. (*pause*) I want to repent. Rabbi. Help me. Help me. I want to repent. Oh, God. Help me.

Pause.

> REBBE
> (*shrugs*)
>
> Come in.

Angle
INS. The door being closed by the Rebbe's hand.

Angle
INT. The house.

The table. The texts are moved.

Angle
The Rebbe motions the Rich Man to sit.

> REBBE
> Sit down. Take off your things. (*pause*) Sit down.

Angle
The Rich Man sits. He rips his hat off.

Angle
The old Rebbe moves to the fire and pokes it up. He puts another small log on the fire. He turns back. He mimes opening his coat.

> REBBE
> Please.

The man opens his coat roughly, revealing a suit of rich material, a large diamond stickpin in his cravat, and a vast gold watchchain.

> RICH MAN
> I want to repent.

The Rebbe moves back from the fire. He fills his glass at the Samovar and puts a small spoonful of jam into it. He motions to the other man, "Would you like some tea…?"

> RICH MAN
> I want to *repent*. I want to *change*. Oh, God. Can you help me, for the love of God… (*he starts to weep*)

The Rebbe sits in the chair opposite the Rich Man.

REBBE
Nu. After all of these years. You want to repent…

RICH MAN
What must I do? Tell me? *Tell* me: money? *Charity*…

The Rebbe shrugs.

RICH MAN
Anything. Anything. Tell me. *Guide* me.

REBBE
You are… *listen* to me: you are not young. Who is to say how much longer you will live? The life you've *chosen*…the *things* you have done…

RICH MAN
I *know*, I *know*.

He stands, and starts tearing off his various ornaments.

RICH MAN
It's *nothing* to me, all I've gained. Take it, *take* it, help me to change. *Help* me…

The Rebbe stands.

REBBE
You're too old to change.

He walks toward the door and looks out the window again.

Angle
His POV: the richly appointed sleigh outside.

Angle
INT. The Rebbe's house.

The Rebbe looking out the window.

> REBBE
> Too much. No.

The Rebbe opens the door to the outside. He turns back.

Angle
His POV: the Rich Man, disheveled, distraught.

Pause.

He starts to pick up his various accoutrements. He walks slowly, utterly dejected, toward the door. He looks back at the Rebbe.

Pause.
He turns away and starts out of the door. As he does so, he reaches up to touch the mezuzah.

Angle
X.C.U. The Rebbe, looking at the Rich Man's hand.

Angle
POV: the Rich Man's hand, touching the mezuzah.

Angle
EXT. The house.

The Rich Man, walking out to his sleigh, the Coachman jumps down to open the door. In the B.G. we see the Rebbe.

> REBBE
> Wait.

Angle
The Rich Man's back.

Pause.

He turns back.

Angle
The Rebbe, as the Rich Man walks back into the shot. The Rebbe shakes his head, uncertain.

> REBBE
> I must study. Make me a list. Of all your sins. (*pause*) Of your whole life. (*pause*) Leave nothing out. Make me that list and bring it to me.

The Rich Man falls on his knees in the snow. He takes the Rebbe's hands and starts to kiss them. The Rebbe raises him to his feet.

> RICH MAN
> Can you, can you...

> REBBE
> I don't know, I don't know. I have to study.

Angle
The Rich Man standing in the snow, his Coachman holding open the door to the sleigh. The Rebbe starts back toward the house.

Angle
INT. The house.

We hear the door close. The Rebbe comes into the room, takes down another candlestick and two new candles, which he lays next to the candlestick. He lights the candle in the candlestick, takes down several volumes from the shelf, and puts them near the candles. He starts to put on his tefillin once again, praying as he does so.

Dissolve.

Angle
INT. Bakery. Day.

A woman carrying out a steaming pitcher of tea.

Angle
EXT. The bakery

The Coachman, stomping his feet. He looks at the woman, hurrying out through the snow. He holds a glass in his hands. She pours the tea into it and gestures with her head, across the way. He shrugs, as if to say, "I have no idea…" He looks back across the way.

Angle
His POV: the Rebbe's house. A bright, snowy day.

Angle
INT. Rebbe's house. Day.

A fire in the grate. Pan off to show the Rebbe, in his chair, wrapped in a shawl. He holds a piece of paper in his hands.

Angle
INS. The piece of paper, covered with closely written handwriting.

Angle
The Rebbe reading. He looks up.

Angle
His POV: sitting across from him sits the Rich Man, now arrayed in a more subdued, plain fashion.

Angle
The Rebbe, gesturing, as if to say, "You did this?"

Angle
The Rich Man he hangs his head and nods sadly.

Angle
The Rebbe sighs. He takes the sheet of paper and lays it to the side.

Angle
The Rich Man, dejected, looking on.

Angle
The Rebbe takes a sheet of paper from an unseen pile to the other side of his desk.

Angle
INS. This pile is five inches thick.

Angle
The Rebbe, as he raises the sheet to his eyes. He rises out of his chair.

>   REBBE
> What! You *did* this…?

Angle
The Rich Man rises out of the chair.

Angle
EXT. The Rebbe's house.

Two shtetl inhabitants walking past turn at the sound and stop, looking toward the Rebbe's window.

Angle
Their POV: through the window we see, but cannot hear clearly, the Rebbe, holding the sheet of paper and screaming at the Rich Man in disbelief.

Angle

The two passers-by, as they listen, watch the scene through the window. Finally the sound subsides.

Angle
INT. The Rebbe's house.

He glares at the whimpering Rich Man, who kneels on the floor, weeping.

Pause.

>   REBBE
>   How can a man do this and live…?

Pause.

The Rich Man shakes his head.

Pause.

The Rebbe goes back behind his desk. He shakes his head. He sits at the desk. He picks up another sheet of paper and sighs.

Angle
EXT. Shtetl. Street. Night.

The dark street, the closed bakery. The Coachman, stomping to keep warm, comes into the shot. He goes to the sleigh and takes out the lap robe, which is covered in snow, to shake it out.

We hear the Rebbe screaming. The Coachman turns.

Angle
His POV: thirty shtetl inhabitants, in the dark, clustered around the fence near the Rebbe's house. Beyond them, the lighted window.

Angle
Pan over their faces, as we hear the Rebbe screaming. Several smile and nudge each other, as if to say, "You see?"

Angle
Over their backs as we see the Rebbe come into the shot, seen through his window, waving a sheaf of papers and screaming in rage.

One of the inhabitants turns to another and shakes her head in sad disbelief.

Beyond them we see the sleigh and the Coachman.

Angle
Sleigh and Coachman, who stomps off again. The Rebbe still screaming.

Angle
EXT. Shtetl. Street. Day.

Several inhabitants, sleeping on their feet, wake with a start at the opening of the Rebbe's door.

Angle
At the door, the Rebbe and the Rich Man.

> REBBE
> You don't want to repent.

> RICH MAN
> Yes. Yes. I do.

> REBBE
> Get out. Get out of my sight. Get out...

He drives the Rich Man out of his door and flings the manuscript after him.

REBBE
Get out! How can you do these things and call yourself a man?

RICH MAN
I want to repent. Rebbe. Help me. I want to.

REBBE
No one can help you.

RICH MAN
What must I do?

REBBE
How can I believe, a man who would do these things would…

RICH MAN
What must I do…?

REBBE
You've cheated, you've lied, you've stolen, you've… I'm not going to *say*, in front of… (*he gestures at the inhabitants*) All of your riches, all of your…

RICH MAN
How can I *prove* to you…

REBBE
Take everything you own. Your houses, your land, your livestock, your jewelry, your clothes, everything but the clothes you wear. Change it into gold, and bring the gold to me. You want to repent? Bring me your ill-gotten gains. Everything. Eh…?

He turns his back on the man. He turns back.

> REBBE
> *(speaking to the townspeople)*
> I think that should dissuade him.

He goes inside the door. Flings out another inch or so of manuscript and slams the door.

Angle.
EXT. The Rebbe's house.

The Rich Man is on his knees in the snow. He looks around.

Angle
The townspeople. They turn away from him and move off.

Angle
The Rich Man, gathering up the pages of his manuscript.

Angle
EXT. Shtetl. Street. Day.

The Rebbe carries a wooden basket with a few vegetables in it, exchanging greetings with a man in the street. He walks round a corner and stops.

Angle
His POV: a crowd, turning to look at him.

Angle
The Rebbe makes his way through the crowd. Beyond it is his house, and in front of his house is the Rich Man's sleigh, piled high with gold. Standing on the doorstep, dressed in a peasant costume, is the Rich Man.

The Rebbe moves through the crowd to him.

Pause.

                    RICH MAN
           All that I own are these clothes.

                      REBBE
           The sleigh.

                    RICH MAN
                    (nodding)
           I gave it to my coachman, and he lent it to
           me.

                      REBBE
           Come in.

Angle
INT. Rebbe's room. Day.

The Rebbe takes a spoonful of jam and puts it into his cup of tea. He brings a cup of tea to the Rich Man, who sits in a chair. The Rebbe moves to his table. On it are piled various texts. All open. The Rebbe sits and makes a note on a thickly scrawled-upon pad. He makes a gesture as if to say, "Ah…" then picks up another text and thumbs through it. He comes to an entry, closes the book, and looks up.

Angle
The Rich Man looks up.

Angle.
The Rebbe comes to him.

                      REBBE
           It's as I thought. I cannot help you.

                    RICH MAN
           How can you doubt me?

REBBE
It is not that I doubt you. I don't doubt
you, but *(he gestures toward the books)* you
are beyond help.

RICH MAN
No. No. You found something.

REBBE
(moving him toward the front door)
I found something, but...

RICH MAN
What?

REBBE
No. I can't help you.

RICH MAN
Anything. Whatever's written. Whatever
I must do to make repentance. Whatever I
must do.

Pause.

Angle
X.C.U. The Rebbe.

REBBE
You must die.

Angle
X.C.U. The Rich Man.

RICH MAN
What?

The Rebbe moves in the shot. Camera pulls back slightly.

REBBE
(softly)
You must die. *(pause)* You must die.

Angle
The Rich Man steps back from the Rebbe.

Pause.

RICH MAN
(very softly)
How must I die?

The Rebbe goes behind his desk. He sighs. He opens a book and makes notes on a sheet of paper. He looks up. He holds the paper out reluctantly.

Angle
The Rich Man steps to the desk and takes the paper. Looks down to read it and nods.

Angle
EXT: Rebbe's house. Night.

The trodden snowpath. Pan up to show the rickety wooden gate. The gate is opened. Beyond it are shtetl inhabitants, racing away from the camera.

Angle
One man, looking on, shakes his head, minutely.

Angle
The backs of the inhabitants. They part to show the Rich Man, covered in a cheap shawl, holding a bundle, moving through the crowd, toward the camera. Behind him is the sleigh, full of gold, now covered in snow.

Angle
His feet, moving slowly, past the open gate. Camera tracks with them through the snow.

Angle
INT. The Rebbe's house.

His table, now cleared. Sound of a knock on the door and the door opening.

Angle
The Rebbe, looking up, as he clears the last few books off the tables. He removes his glass of tea and the pot of jam behind him. A large fire in the grate. The Rebbe bends and puts yet another log on the fire.

Angle
The fire, blazing up, as the Rebbe feeds it.

Hold on the fire.

> REBBE
> You don't have to continue.

> RICH MAN
> I must.

Angle
The Rich Man and the Rebbe. The Rich Man holds a bundle.

> REBBE
> If there were any other way...

The Rich Man nods, understanding.

Pause.

The Rebbe looks around. He sighs and motions the Rich Man to stand still. The Rebbe moves to his tefillin box on the mantle next to the tea and the pot of jam. He puts on his tefillin and starts to pray.

Angle
The Rich Man. Standing alone in the room, he looks up as the Rebbe stops praying.

Angle
His POV: the Rebbe, now covering himself with a tallis, and praying again. The Rebbe now moves to the man and takes the bundle which the man holds. He motions, and the man, not understanding at first, then holds out the sheet which the Rebbe had given him previously. The Rebbe looks down at the sheet and nods, as he reads it. He puts the small bundle on the mantle.

> REBBE
> Are you sure you want to continue.

Angle
C.U. The Rich Man.

He nods.

Angle
The Rebbe.

> REBBE
> Lay on the table. Please. Head near the fire.
> On your back. With your head near the
> fire.

The Rich Man does so. The Rebbe opens the bundle and takes out a ladle. He looks at the ladle. The Rebbe looks into the bundle.

> REBBE
> Where is the bar of lead?

The Rich Man half-rises, pats his pockets, and hands the Rebbe a small bar of lead.

Angle
INS. The small lead bar as the Rebbe takes it. Camera moves with the bar to the fire where the Rebbe puts it into the ladle and places the ladle in the fire.

Angle
The Rebbe comes over and stands by the Rich Man, who now lies with his back on the table again.

He looks down at the Rich Man, who closes his eyes and starts to pray. The Rebbe looks down at him.

Pause.

The Rebbe puts his hand on the Rich Man's shoulder.

REBBE
I'm sorry.

X.C.U. The Rich Man. looks up and nods and begins praying again.

Angle
The Rebbe, standing by the head of the Rich Man. He looks over at the fire.

Angle
His POV: the ladle. The lead is melting.

Angle
The Rebbe looks at the Rich Man, sighs, and moves past him to the windows.

Angle
EXT. The Rebbe's house.

The shtetl inhabitants looking on.

Angle
The Coachman, holding the horse, now wearing saddle and bridle.

Angle
Two old women, looking on, draw a sharp breath.

Angle
Their POV: the shutters of the Rebbe's house being closed.

Angle
Several older people starting to pray.

Angle
The Coachman, hanging his head.

Angle
INT. The Rebbe's house.

He moves to the opposite shutters and closes them. He stops by the fire and looks down.

Angle
His POV: the ladle. All the lead is melted and is bubbling.

Angle
The Rebbe, as he sighs and bends down to take the ladle, thinks at the last minute, and removes a large handkerchief from his back pocket and uses it to pick up the ladle.

Angle
EXT. The Rebbe's house.

The inhabitants, some praying. One man standing still, then hurriedly takes out a prayerbook from his back pocket and begins praying.

Angle
The Rich Man on the table. The Rebbe behind him, in front of the fire.

                    REBBE
                   (softly)
        You must move down, and hang your head
        over.

The Rich Man nods and does so. He turns his head slightly to look.

Angle
His POV: the ladle, glowing, the lead bubbling, being raised toward him.

Angle
The Rebbe and the Rich Man. As he turns back

                    REBBE
                   (softly)
        God bless you. I'm sorry.

The Rich Man nods and begins praying again. He scrintches up his face.

Angle
The Rebbe, moving closer, with the ladle.

                    REBBE
                   (softly)
        You must open your mouth.

The Rich Man does so.

                    REBBE
        God, grant repentance to this man, and us
        all.

Angle
X.C.U. The Rich Man's face in profile as the ladle is brought close to it. His face begins to glow from the heat. The volume of his prayers increases.

Angle
The Rebbe, bringing the ladle closer.

Angle
The Rich Man's face.

Angle
Just the Rebbe's hand, holding the ladle handle, as it comes close to the face. The Rich Man opens his mouth wider.

Angle
The Rebbe's hand coming down.

Angle
The Rebbe's face, as a huge scream is heard.

Angle
The inhabitants, looking up in terror, as the scream is heard.

Angle
INT. The Rebbe's house.

The Rich Man sits up with a jolt, still screaming in terror. He has a spoon in his mouth. He gradually stops screaming, feels in his mouth, and takes out the spoon. He looks wonderingly at the Rebbe. He looks down at the spoon.

The Rebbe walks to the fire and replaces the full ladle on the hearth floor.

He walks to the Rich Man, who takes the spoon out of his mouth and looks at it. The Rebbe takes the spoon and wipes it on the handkerchief. He goes to the mantle and replaces it into the pot of jam.

Angle
The Rich Man, sitting on the table. The Rebbe comes back to him. The Rebbe puts his hands on the man's shoulders and looks at him.

Angle
EXT. The Rebbe's house.
His door opens and he comes out with the Rich Man. They walk into the little yard. The Rich Man still in shock. The Rebbe covers him with the shawl he takes off his own shoulders. The Rich Man looks around in wonder. He turns back to the Rebbe.

RICH MAN
I just want to be a good man.

REBBE
That's not given us to know. (*pause*) Be a good *Jew*.

He turns the Rich Man around.

REBBE
Now, go and do better with your gold.

The Rebbe turns and starts back toward his own house.

Angle
The Rich Man, moving through the crowd of inhabitants. Smiling, he stops to shake one and another by the hand.

Angle
C.U. The Rich Man smiles and licks his lips. He raises a finger and wipes some jam off of his lips. He licks the jam off.

Angle
INT. The Rebbe's house.

He opens the shutters, looks out the window. He sits, taking a book with him, and puts it on the table in front of him. He sighs and opens the book, which thwaps loudly on the table.

Dissolve.

INT. The plane. The thwapping sound continues.

Pan onto the face of the Old Man in the back of the plane.

He fidgets a bit, looks forward, his face growing concerned.

Angle
The Officer, coming awake. The flight deck is full of light.

The Officer squints, turns to the Sergeant.

> OFFICER
> Ran the tank dry. Switch to the regular tank. I've got it.

The Officer takes the controls. We hear the sound of the engines sputtering.

Angle
The Old Man and the Sergeant.

> OLD MAN
> What is it?

> SERGEANT
> The extra tank that we installed is empty. We're switching to the plane's main tanks.

He looks around. He sees the fuel-cock, marked "PETROL, MAIN TANK, OPEN/CLOSED."

Angle
INS. The switch, as he throws it to "OPEN."

Angle
The Sergeant, as he moves back to the cockpit.

> SERGEANT
> Nothing to it. Just like a B-25.

He drops back into the right-hand seat.

> SERGEANT
> We should be making landfall in three, maybe four…

Sound of an engine sputtering. The Sergeant looks to his right.

Angle
His POV: the sea, the bright sky, and the engine stopping.

Angle
INT. Cockpit.

> SERGEANT
> Lost the starboard.

> OFFICER
> Feather it, what's the…

Sound of another engine sputtering. The Officer looks to his left.

Angle
His POV: the port engine, stopping.

Angle
INT. Cockpit

> OFFICER
> Oh hell…

He bends to the controls.

Angle
His POV: the controls. Fuel gauge reads "MAIN TANK, FULL."

> SERGEANT (V.O.)
> What is it?

> OFFICER
> We ain't getting the fuel. It's not…

Angle
The two men on the flight deck.

> OFFICER
> Oh Mary. Not *now*…

> SERGEANT
> The main tank's full. They topped it off, I saw it.

> OFFICER
> Check the connection.

Angle
EXT. The plane.

A stretch of sky, and the plane, falling silently, through it.

Angle
INT. The cargo area.

The Old Man moves out of the way as the Sergeant comes back into the area. We see the Old Man fidgeting.

> SERGEANT
> I don't even have… I ditched my *wrench*, when we…

He looks forward.

Angle
The Officer, trying various switches, forward.

                    OFFICER
            Check the, check…

Angle
The Old Man. He looks down at the clipboard. He reads, as the colloquy between the Officer and the Sergeant continues. He looks up.

                    OLD MAN
            Is this…?

Angle
The Sergeant looks back.

                    SERGEANT
            What?

                    OLD MAN
            Is this… (*he gestures at the clipboard*)

                    SERGEANT
            Is this "what"? What is… What…

He takes the clipboard and reads.

Angle
INS. The Clipboard. It reads: "R.A.F. Brindisi. Maintenance report."

Angle
The Officer.

                    OFFICER
            Okay. Prepare to ditch. If those tanks *are*
            full, she's gonna blow when we hit the
            water. If not… Did you jettison the rafts..?
            Hey… Did you…

Angle
Back in the cargo area. The Sergeant, reading the maintenance report. Beyond him, the Officer.

                    OFFICER
    We're gonna *ditch* it. Do we have the rafts?

The Sergeant looks up.

Angle
His POV.

INS. The fuel cock reads: "PETROL, MAIN TANK, OPEN/CLOSED." The lever is on "OPEN." The Sergeant's hand moves it to "CLOSED."

Angle
The Sergeant, looking at the fuel cock. We hear the Officer screaming and then the sound of the engines kicking in.

Angle
On the flight deck. The Officer looks out at the engines as they come to life.

Anglc
His POV: the port engine, not spinning.

Angle
INT. The plane.

The Officer manipulating the controls.

Angle
EXT. The plane.

The plane rising toward the camera, away from the sea.

Angle
INT. The plane.

The Officer looks back.

Angle
Behind him. The two others. The Sergeant gestures at the clipboard.

> SERGEANT.
> They installed the fuel cutoff backwards...

Angle
INS. The fuel cutoff, now reading "CLOSED."

The Sergeant's head comes into the shot.

> SERGEANT
> That's why she was in the shop. (*to the Old Man*) Thank you.

Angle
The Old Man begins to take off his coat. He shrugs. He looks out of the window.

Angle
Back on the flight deck. The Sergeant settling back into his seat.

> SERGEANT
> How we doing?

The Officer shrugs.

> OFFICER
> We got enough fuel to make land, then all we got to do is not come down on the wrong side of this war. Find us an airstrip and I'll buy you a beer.

The Sergeant starts taking off his British tunic. He does so and takes the controls. The Officer strips off his tunic.

OFFICER
Me, I could go for a glass of milk.

SERGEANT
Milk, that's a hideous substance.

OFFICER
Not by me.

They both squint in the bright sun.

OFFICER
We got any sunglasses? I can't see all.

SERGEANT
Just keep her on the compass. Keep heading east… *(softly to himself)*…Into the midst of another war… Keep heading east…

Angle
C.U. The Officer as he squints.

Angle
His POV: the compass, reading 85 degrees.

Angle
The Officer.

OFFICER
(to himself)
A glass of ice-cold milk.

Pause.

OLD MAN (V.O.)
In our village. (*pause*) There was a man. (*pause*) There was a man, and he had a goat.

Camera pans over the cockpit, past the Officer, past the Old Man in the back, past the Sergeant, who is hunched down in his seat, eyes closed.

> OLD MAN (V.O.)
> He had a goat.

Dissolve.

> OLD MAN (V.O.)
> And this goat gave the finest milk.

Angle
EXT. Shtetl. Summer.

A rundown hut. A man chopping wood.

> OLD MAN (V.O.)
> This man was very poor. He had two things in the world. The goat, and his son.

The man looks up.

Angle
Hs POV: a group of barefoot young boys, carrying books, walking down the dirt road. One Boy peels off of the group. Camera pans him, past the rough picket fence, where we see the goat enclosed, and into the yard, where his father hugs him. The Boy proceeds inside the hut.

Angle
INT. The hut.

The Boy puts his books on the table of the dirt-floored hut. Opens a notebook and a book, takes a pencil from his pocket, makes a note in the notebook.

Angle
EXT. The hut.

The Woodchopper, still chopping wood. The Boy emerges holding a pail. As he comes out, he puts the pencil in his pocket.

Dissolve.

Angle
EXT. The hut. Sundown.

The Woodchopper stacking the wood against his house. He turns back toward the camera.

> OLD MAN (V.O.)
> What a strange thing is fame.

> MAN'S VOICE (V.O.)
> Hey, Yussel. How much for your goat?

The Woodchopper smiles.

Angle
A shtetl inhabitant, his horse and cart stopped by the fence, drinking from a tin cup. Inside the fence are the Boy, who is seated on a milking stool by the goat, and the goat. The Boy slaps the goat on the rump and the goat gambols away, leaving the Boy near the pail of milk.

Angle
The Boy, going into the house with the pail of milk, in the B.G. The Cart Man drinking. The Woodchopper comes up to the Cart Man.

> CART MAN
> I tell you, it makes my trip worthwhile,
> every time. I come, just to have some of
> that milk.

He fishes in his vest and gives a small coin to the Woodchopper.

                      CART MAN
            But I suppose they all say that.

                      WOODCHOPPER
            Indeed they do.

The Cart Man finishes the milk, wipes out the cup, and hangs it on his belt. He moves around to the cart and gets up on it. He calls down.

                      CART MAN
            If you could find out what the goat *eats*…
            Do you know, you could make a *fortune*.

Angle
The Cart Man driving off. The Woodchopper in the B.G., in the setting sun.

                      WOODCHOPPER
            What he *eats*…? (*he gestures around him*)
            He eats what *any* of them eat. It's, it's, it's
            something special in the, I don't know, the
            goat is special…

Hold.

Dissolve.

Angle
INT. The hut. Night.

A lit oil lamp. Pan onto the Woodchopper, who is sitting, pensive.

Angle
Beyond him. The Boy, cleaning up the dishes. The Boy comes back to the table. He puts his books on the table, opens a notebook, takes the pencil out of his pocket, and starts to write.

Pause.

He looks up.

Angle
The Boy and his father. The father feels the son's gaze and looks up at him.

Pause.

> WOODCHOPPER
> If we could find out what the goat *eats*…

> BOY
> What he eats. He eats what any of them eat.

> WOODCHOPPER
> But *does* he…? (*pause*) Eh?

The Woodchopper nods at his own sagacity.

> WOODCHOPPER
> *Does* he…

He messes up the Boy's hair, kisses him, and sits down and begins to fill his pipe.

Pause.

He looks up at the Boy and nods. He turns.

Angle
POV: out of the window. The goat walks across the frame.

Angle
The Woodchopper and the Boy in the room.

Dissolve.

Angle
EXT. The hut. Morning.

A group of students, holding their books, walking. A couple of them look back.

Angle.
Their POV: the Woodchopper's hut and the Woodchopper's son standing with his back to the camera.

Angle
The Woodchopper's son looking on.

Angle
His POV: the far side of the fence. The open gate, the goat grazing. The goat wanders out of the yard.

Angle
In the house. The Woodchopper, looking out of the window, watches the goat wandering out of the yard and out into a field.

Angle
The Boy, standing near the hut, watching the goat. The Woodchopper nods to the Boy, who turns and begins to follow the goat.

Angle
EXT. Hillside.

The goat, his bell jingling, grazing. The goat looks back.

Angle
The Boy, coming up the hillside, the shtetl down below him.

Angle
EXT. The hut.
The Woodchopper, coming out, looks up the hillside, smiles, rubs his hands together.

Angle
His POV: the hillside. The Boy and the goat just dots, moving up the hill.

Angle
EXT. Rickety bridge. Day.

Pan over to a dilapidated haywagon moving onto the bridge, where we see the Boy looking down.

Angle
The wagon, as it moves on. A Cossack on a sleek horse comes galloping past. Those on the wagon make an obeisance. The driver looks back.

Angle
His POV: the Cossack galloping over the bridge. The Boy on the bridge.

Angle
The Boy's POV: the goat, down below, on the stream. The goat, grazing, looks up and moves off.

Angle
The Boy, coming down the embankment, the bridge behind him, moving toward the camera. Tilt down to reveal the goat, which moves out of frame, again leaving the Boy.

Angle
EXT. A steep hillside.

The Boy, coming up the hill, to camera. Panting. He stops to wipe his brow. He listens.

Pause.

He moves through the trees.

Pause.

He looks around. He sits. Distracted. He tries to control his breath.

Pause.

He hears the small tinkle of the goat's bell. He gets to his feet. He looks around. He hears the bell again. He starts off up the hill.

Angle
A rocky precipice. The goat comes into the shot.

Angle
Down below, the Boy, looking up.

Angle
EXT. Rocky hillside.

Hold. The Boy comes into the shot. He is cold and hugs himself to keep warm. He looks around.

Angle.
His POV: on another precipice, some ways away, stands the goat.

Angle
The other precipice. The goat comes into the shot. We see the Boy down below, working his way over the rocks.

Angle
The Boy, maneuvering over the rocks.

Angle
His feet, searching for purchase on the narrow rocky ledge. The sound of the goat's bell.

Angle
The Boy looks down.

Angle
POV: his feet, kicking loose stones, and a sheer drop. His feet move out of the shot.

Angle
The Boy, safe on the rocky outcropping.

Pause.

He stops. Listening. There is no sound of the bell.

Angle
The camera follows the boy around the outcropping. There is no sound of the bell. The boy stands, confused. He sits. Shivering.

Pause.

He turns behind him.

Angle
His POV: the small opening of a cave. The Boy crawls into the shot. We hear the goat's bell tinkling in the distance.

Angle
INT. The cave.

The Boy's head and the sky outside. The Boy starts into the cave.

Angle
INT. A cavern in the cave.

Sound of wind whistling through the cave. The Boy can straighten up inside the cavern. He looks around. Again he hears the sound of the bell and moves with the camera to an opening in the cavern, and, again, begins to crawl.

Dissolve.

Angle
INT. The tunnel in the cave.

The Boy, wide-eyed and filthy, crawling on. He stops. He catches his breath. He hears the bell and moves on.

Angle
The floor of the tunnel. The boy's bloody hand comes into the frame and pulls his body on. Camera pans up to the Boy's face. He stops. He listens. There is no sound. The Boy starts to cry. He cries for a moment, then sighs, and reaches forward. He stops, looking perplexed.

Angle
Another cavern. The Boy's hand coming out of the tunnel. There is a shaft of light across his hand.

Angle
In the tunnel, the Boy pulls himself forward. Light falls on his face as he comes out of the tunnel.

Angle
INT. A cavern, half filled with light.

The Boy stands up, dirty and bloody. He looks around. He looks up.

Angle
His POV: a slight rise, a natural ramp, above which we see blue sky. The Boy starts to move up the ramp.

Angle
The mouth of the ramp, on a green hill. The Boy comes out of the cavern. He looks amazed. He moves forward and rests by a tree, which shades the entrance of the cavern. He looks at the tree with astonishment.

Angle
His POV: the tree is a date palm. The Boy moves into the shot. He hears the tinkling of the bell and turns to look.

Angle
POV: a lush oasis, ringed with palms. A caravan of three men on camels moving away from the oasis. As they move, we see the goat cropping the grass.

Angle
The Boy coming down the hill. He stops by the water, drinks, and looks up at the goat.

The Boy bathes his face. He looks up again at the goat.

Dissolve.

Angle
EXT. Oasis. Evening.

A date palm. The Boy, dressed in pants only, his body now clean, comes over past the palm, where we now see the goat grazing.

The Boy walks over to his clothes, now clean, which are lying, drying on the grass. He dresses himself. He follows the goat past several trees. The Boy reaches up and takes some fruit off of one of the trees.

He follows the goat to the edge of the hill, below which we see a vast, fertile valley spreading, and beyond that, a blue sea. The Boy sits and watches the sea.

Hold.
He hears the tinkling of the goat's bell. He turns.

Angle
His POV: the goat has started back up the hill and has turned back to look at the Boy.

Angle
The Boy gets up and walks to the goat. He stands by the goat and looks back at the sea. He takes the pencil from his pocket and looks around. He tears the tail from his shirt and sits on

the ground and writes, placing the torn piece of fabric on a rock. He finishes writing and rolls up the fabric tightly. He moves to the goat. He bends.

Angle
Tight on the goat's head, as the Boy holds him by the collar and puts the rolled-up message into the goat's ear.

Angle
The Boy and the goat. The Boy slaps the goat on the rump.

BOY
Go, now… Go home.

He claps his hands and the goat runs off, up the hillside.

Angle
EXT. The entrance of the cave.

The goat comes into the shot and exits. Down below we see the Boy.

Angle
C.U. The Boy sitting, looking out to sea, the breeze blowing his clothes.

Hold.

Dissolve.
EXT. Woodchopper's house. Dusk.

Angle
INS. A block of wood. The maul comes down on it, and it splits.

Pause.
Another block is put on the chopping block. The maul comes down, and it splits.

Angle
The head and upper torso of the Woodchopper as he raises the maul. He hears the tinkling of the goat's bell. He smiles. He lowers his maul.

Angle
The Woodchopper standing, the house beside him, as he gazes. Smiling, he shades his eyes.

Angle
His POV: the goat, coming down the hill.

Angle
The Woodchopper, shading his eyes, still looking.

Angle
The empty hillside.

Dissolve.

Angle
INT. Woodchopper's house. Night.

A plate of soup steaming on the table. Pan over to reveal another steaming plate of soup next to it. Continue to pan to show the back of the Woodchopper's head as he gazes out the window at the dark hillside.

Dissolve.

INT. Woodchopper's house. Night.

A slant of moonlight across the table. The two non-steaming bowls of soup. Tilt up to show the moon seen through the window.

Angle
EXT. Woodchopper's house. Night.

The Woodchopper, standing in the moonlight, looking at the hill. Hold. He hears the tinkling of the goat bell. He turns slowly.

Angle
The goat, grazing quietly in the yard, lifts its head.
Dissolve.

Sun glinting off the handle of an axe which leans by the feet of the Woodchopper.

Angle
The Woodchopper, head in his hands, sitting on the chopping block. He raises his head to look up at the hillside.

Angle
His POV: the empty hillside. The Woodchopper stands into the shot. We see his back.

Angle
The front of the hut. The goat grazing. The Woodchopper comes around one side of the hut as the goat disappears around the other.

Angle
INT. The hut.

The books of the Boy.

Hold.

The Woodchopper's hands lovingly pick them up.

Angle
The Woodchopper, carrying the books. He puts them on the Boy's bed. He stands in the middle of the room and looks out of the window.

Angle
His POV: the empty hillside.

Hold.

The goat comes into the shot, tinkling his bell.

Angle
X.C.U. The Woodchopper, resolute.

Angle
EXT. The yard.

The goat, grazing. Walks past the block, against which the axe rests. The goat leaves the shot.

Angle.
The legs of the Woodchopper coming toward the block.

Angle
The goat grazing.

Angle
The axe head. The Woodchopper's hand comes into the frame and picks it up.

Angle
The goat, in close up, looking back.

Angle
The back of Woodchopper, as he advances on the goat, who retreats into a corner of the fence.

Angle
The Woodchopper advances on the goat, reaches down, and grabs the goat by the collar. The goat starts bleating. The Woodchopper drags the goat toward the block.

> WOODCHOPPER
> Because of you. Because of you…

Angle
The chopping block.

> WOODCHOPPER (V.O.)
> You killed the only thing I love.

The goat's head is placed on the block.

Angle
The head and shoulders of the man, the goat bleating. The man brings up the maul and brings it down and we hear a dull thud.

Angle
The goat, lying stunned, its head on the block.

Angle
The man, lifting the axe above his head.

> WOODCHOPPER
> You killed my son.

Angle
Sound of the axe head, in the air, being raised, then brought down. The axe severing the goat's head.

Angle
The man, standing by the chopping block. Rests his axe against the block.

> WOODCHOPPER
> *(to himself)*
> You killed my son.

He looks down.

Angle
The severed goat's head.

Angle
The Woodchopper spits at it and kicks it as he starts back into his house.

Angle
The goat's head flops over.

Angle
The Woodchopper, walking back to the house, glances back at the goat's head

Hold.

Angle
The goat's head in the foreground. The Woodchopper beyond it, walking back.

Angle
The Woodchopper, bending down. Reaches for something.

Angle
X.C.U. The goat's ear, the small piece of cloth. The Woodchopper's hand picks out the small piece of cloth and starts to unroll it.

Angle
The Woodchopper, reading the small piece of cloth.

Angle
INS. His hands, holding the cloth, on which we see written: "Follow the goat."

Angle
From the road. The Woodchopper, holding the note. The carcass of the goat. A large haywagon comes into the foreground of the shot and obliterates the scene. Camera pans with the haywagon and up to two teenage girls, driving it, laughing musically.

Dissolve.

INT. The plane.

The laughter mixes with the drone of the engines.

In the cargo compartment of the plane.

Panning back over the fuel cock, to the face of the Old Man, who is tired, speaking slowly, looking out the window.

> OLD MAN
> *(to himself)*
> And one man. One man... One unlearned man, came to the shul each day. Every year. Each day. With a sack. And he took objects from the sack, and mumbled over them. One day the Rebbe asked him what they were, and they were children's building blocks. With Hebrew letters. And he said he did not know the prayers. All he knew were the letters. But he said them, and knew God would put them together for him, knowing what was in his heart.

Angle
Cockpit. The Officer's face. Red-eyed, sweaty. He checks his watch. Looks to his right.

Angle
The face of the Sergeant, who glances down at the control panel.

Angle
INS. The fuel gauge, the needle resting just above empty.

Angle
The two men glance at each other.

> OFFICER
> *(sighs)*
> Well...

                        SERGEANT
               Land! Land! I see it!

Angle
His POV: a coastline. A mountain to the left.

Angle
The two men in the cockpit, jubilant. They look back at the
Old Man, who nods.

                        OFFICER
               Okay, where are we…?

The Sergeant consults some figures on a pad.

                        SERGEANT
               I figure… with the crosswind… we're
               south. Make the coast…

                        OFFICER
               We're south…

                        SERGEANT
               We have to be. Make the coast, and come
               left…

                        OFFICER
               Left…

                        SERGEANT
               We're… You turn right, you're taking us
               into *Egypt.* Cross the coast, turn left, and
               look for a strip.

The Officer nods.

                        OFFICER
                     (to the Old Man)
               Well, there it is, Papa. There it is. Palestine.

OFFICER
The land of Israel.

OLD MAN
When you cross the coastline, you must turn south. *South.* To the left. Not north.

SERGEANT
Okay. We'll fly the plane.

OLD MAN
South.

SERGEANT
You been here before?

The Old Man shakes his head. He points.

OLD MAN
That is Mount *Carmel.* That is Mount Carmel. Mount Carmel is in the *north.* Ahab brought Elijah up to Mount Carmel. Up. It is in the north. If you turn north, away from it.

OFFICER
Mount Carmel's in the north.

OLD MAN
Of course. (*pause*) There was a mighty wind. The Lord was not in the wind. An earthquake. But he was not there. And then a fire. He was not in the fire, but after the fire…

SERGEANT
What if…

                    OFFICER
     Let him talk.

                    OLD MAN
     And the Lord said: go on to Damascus.
     North of Mount Carmel is Damascus…

Pause.

                    OFFICER
     What if that's not Mount Carmel?

Angle
The Sergeant, figuring on his pad.

                    SERGEANT
                  (shakes his head)
     You got to turn north… *(he gestures to his
     pad)* F'you turn south, we're in Egypt, in a
     plane with a Star of David on the wing…

Angle
The three men, seen from the front of the cockpit.

                    OFFICER
     What if that's not Mount Carmel?

Sound of an engine missing. The officer looks down.

Angle
His POV: the fuel gauge. The needle resting on main tank: EMPTY. The engine quits.

Angle
The three men in the cockpit. The engine catches again.

Angle
EXT. The plane.

From above, the plane crosses the coastline.

Angle
INT. Cockpit.

> SERGEANT
> Turn *left*...Turn *left*... For God's sake, Danny...

Angle
C.U. The Officer. He turns back.

Angle
His POV: the Old Man, signaling with his hand "turn right."

Angle
The Officer. He turns the wheel.

> OFFICER
> No, I'm going to the right...

Angle
EXT. The plane. It veers to the right.

Angle
The land. Desert. Some coastal scrub. Someone shades his eyes and looks up at the plane.

Angle
INT. The plane.

Cockpit. The engines quit again. The Officer and the Sergeant look at each other. The Sergeant, looking out the window.

> SERGEANT
> I got a strip, I got a strip, I got a landing strip!

Angle
His POV: a small landing strip.

Angle
The men in the cockpit.

> OFFICER
> Oh Lord, let them be ours.
>
> SERGEANT
> I don't even got the gun, Danny, I tossed the gun out…

Sound: the engine quits. The Officer wiggles the controls.

The engines sputters once or twice.

Angle
EXT. The small control shed. Desert airfield.

Two people at a small machine gun, the plane in the distance. They clamber around in the gun and track the plane.

Angle
EXT. The plane, banking for an approach.

Angle
INT. The plane.

We see the plane, banking, onto the final approach.

Angle
On the ground. The two machine gunners.

Angle
The finger of one starts to tighten on the trigger.

> MACHINE GUNNER
> *Hinei!*

Angle
On the ground. The Machine gunner stands up. The other Machine gunner is pointing at the plane. They shade their eyes to look at it.

Angle
In the plane. The Officer and the Sergeant. The engine quits. Sound of wind whistling. The Officer wiggles the controls.

> OFFICER
> That's it. Wherever we are, here we are, we're coming in dead stick…

Angle
A hillside, the field down below, the sea beyond it. A young woman soldier carrying a rifle slung, in the foreground. In the B.G. is the plane, lined up on final approach and gliding down.

Angle
Cockpit.

> SERGEANT
> *(looking out the window)*
> We're here, we're here, we made it.

Angle
His POV: the Israeli flag flying over the shed.

Angle
INT. The plane.

The Officer and the Sergeant.

> OFFICER
> We're going to come in hard. Tell the old man to hold on.

The Sergeant turns to the back.

Angle
EXT. The plane, coming down, the Star of David painted under its wing.

Angle
INT. The plane.

X.C.U. The Sergeant, turned back toward the cargo hold. He turns back to look at the officer.

Pause.

> SERGEANT
> There's no one there.

Pause.

Angle
The Officer and the Sergeant. The Officer shoots a quick glance at the Sergeant.

Angle
Behind them. From the front. We see the Officer and the Sergeant and the empty cargo hold.

Angle
At the small control shed, several people moving toward the runway.

Angle
EXT. Hillside.

The female soldier, the plane below, just touching down. A pan takes the camera behind a slight rise, so we see only the hillside and the sea beyond. Camera continues to pan onto a goat grazing on the hill.

End.